School Union Deseret Sunday

Questions and Answers on the Life and Mission

Of the Prophet Joseph Smith

School Union Deseret Sunday

Questions and Answers on the Life and Mission
Of the Prophet Joseph Smith

ISBN/EAN: 9783337054502

Printed in Europe, USA, Canada, Australia, Japan

Cover: Foto ©Lupo / pixelio.de

More available books at **www.hansebooks.com**

DESERET SUNDAY SCHOOL CATECHISM NO. 1.

QUESTIONS AND ANSWERS

ON THE

LIFE AND MISSION

OF THE

PROPHET JOSEPH SMITH.

PUBLISHED BY THE

DESERET SUNDAY SCHOOL UNION.

JUVENILE INSTRUCTOR OFFICE,
Salt Lake City, Utah.
1882.

PREFACE.

THE Deseret Sunday School Union takes pleasure in presenting to its friends and co-workers this little volume of QUESTIONS AND ANSWERS ON THE LIFE AND MISSION OF JOSEPH SMITH, the great Prophet of the latter-day dispensation.

Great care has been taken by the Publishing Committee to avoid errors, but should any appear, every effort will be made to correct them in future editions.

Necessarily, in a work of this size many items of much value have been left out. If everything had been inserted that might interest the Saints, the volume would have been so large as to be unsuitable for the purpose intended, and the cost so high as to limit its circulation.

It may be well to add that all the literary labor, compilation, etc., has been done by members of the Committee, without charge or payment of any kind, and any profit that may arise from its publication will be devoted by the Union to the preparation and publication of still other works, for which there is a demand among the laborers in our Sunday schools.

Salt Lake City, June 1, 1882.

CONTENTS.

CHAPTER I.

CHAPTER II.

CHAPTER III.

CHAPTER IV.

CHAPTER V.

CHAPTER VI.

QUESTIONS AND ANSWERS

ON THE LIFE OF

JOSEPH SMITH, THE PROPHET.

CHAPTER I.

ONLY ONE TRUE CHURCH—JOSEPH SMITH'S BIRTH AND BOY-
HOOD—HIS PRAYER ANSWERED—GOD, THE FATHER, AND
HIS SON, JESUS CHRIST, APPEAR—VISIT FROM THE
ANGEL MORONI.

1 Q.—Is there more than one Church of God on the earth?
A.—No; there is but one true Church.

2 Q.—What is its name?
A.—The Church of Jesus Christ of Latter-day Saints.

3 Q.—Who gave it this name?
A.—It was revealed. or made known by God.

4 Q.—To whom was this revelation given?
A.—To Joseph Smith.

5 Q.—Who was Joseph Smith?
A - A prophet whom God raised up to begin His great
work in our days.

6 Q.—When was Joseph Smith born?
A.—On the 23rd of December. 1805.

7 Q.--Where was he born?
A - -At Sharon, Windsor County, in the State of Ver-
mont.

8 Q.—What were his parents' names?
A.—Joseph and Lucy Smith.

9 Q.—What took place in the neighborhood where Joseph
ved when he was a little over fourteen years old?
A.—A revival of religion.

10 Q.—What is meant by a religious revival?

A.—Different ministers get up a religious excitement, preach, pray and hold camp meetings.

11 Q.—Did Joseph go to any of these revival meetings?

A.—Yes; and it made him think much about religion.

12 Q.—Did he join any of the sects who were holding these meetings?

A.—No; because he did not know which one was right.

13 Q.—Did Joseph read the Bible?

A.—Yes, often.

14 Q.—What particular passage attracted his attention?

A.—The words of the Apostle James, wherein he says, "If any of you lack wisdom, let him ask of God," etc.

15 Q.—Did Joseph need wisdom?

A.—Yes; for he wanted to serve God very much, but did not know the right way.

16 Q.—What did Joseph determine to do?

A.—To ask God, in prayer, what course he should take.

17 Q.—How old was Joseph at that time?

A.—Between fourteen and fifteen years old.

18 Q.—Where did he go to pray?

A.—He went into a grove of trees not far from his father's house.

19 Q:—What did he ask God?

A.—Which of the religious sects was right.

20 Q.—Did he receive an answer to his prayer?

A.—Yes; for he asked in faith, believing that the words of the Bible were true.

21 Q.—Who appeared to him at this time?

A.—God, the Father, and His Son, Jesus Christ.

22 Q.—What did the Father say?

A.—"This is my beloved Son, hear Him."

23 Q.—What did the Lord tell Joseph about the religious sects?

A.—That not one of them was His church, and that he was to join none of them.

24 Q.—What else did the Lord say about these sects?

A.—That they had a form of godliness, but denied th power thereof.

25 Q.—What promise was then made to Joseph by the Lord?

A.—That the true gospel should be made known to him in due time.

26 Q.—When did Joseph have this glorious vision of the Father and Son?

A.—Early in the spring of 1820.

27 Q.—Who next appeared to Joseph?

A.—The angel Moroni.

28 Q.—Who was Moroni?

A.—An ancient Nephite prophet.

29 Q.—Where and when did Moroni live?

A.—He lived upon this continent between fourteen and fifteen hundred years ago.

30 Q.—When did the Angel Moroni appear to Joseph?

A.—During the night of the 21st of September, 1823.

31 Q.—How old was Joseph at that time?

A.—Nearly eighteen years.

32 Q.—How many visits did the angel make during the night?

A.—He appeared to him three times.

33 Q.—What did the angel say about the fullness of the gospel?

A.—That it would soon be revealed and preached in power.

34 Q.—What did the angel tell Joseph about the work he would have to do?

A.—That he was called and chosen by God, to bring about His mighty purposes.

35 Q.—What did the angel tell him regarding a certain sacred book?

A.—That it was engraved on plates and buried in the ground.

36 Q.—Of whom did this book give an account?

A.—Of the people who lived on the continent of America in ancient days.

37 Q.—What else did it contain?

A.—The fullness of the everlasting gospel, as taught by Jesus to the people upon this land.

38 Q.—What were these people called to whom Jesus delivered His gospel?

A.—The Nephites.

39 Q.—Why were they called Nephites?

A.—Because their first ruler was named Nephi.

40 Q.—Where was this sacred book buried?

A.—In a hill called Cumorah.

41 Q.—Where is the hill Cumorah?

A.—Near the village of Manchester, in Ontario County, in the State of New York.

CHAPTER II.

VISIT TO THE HILL CUMORAH—THE PLATES OBTAINED—WAY-LAID—PERSECUTED—TRANSLATION OF PLATES COM-MENCED.

1 Q.—Did the angel show Joseph the place where the plates were buried?

A.—Yes; and he saw it so plainly that he easily found it the next day.

2 Q.—What were hidden with the plates?

A.—The Urim and Thummim and a breastplate.

3 Q.—Who met Joseph at the hill Cumorah?

A.—Moroni.

4 Q.—How often did Joseph meet Moroni at the hill Cumorah before he received the plates?

A.—On the 22nd of each September until 1827.

5 Q.—When were the plates delivered to Joseph?

A.—On the 22nd of September, 1827.

6 Q.—How were the plates buried in the ground?

A.—In a stone box, the top of which was rounded.

7 Q.—What did Joseph do with the plates?

A —He took them home with great care.

8 Q.—Why were these plates hidden in the earth?

A.—To keep them from being destroyed by wicked men.

9 Q.—Who hid them?

A.—Moroni; he who gave them to Joseph.

10 Q.—How old was Joseph when he received the plates?

A.—Twenty-one years.

11 Q.—What caution did the angel give to Joseph?

A.—He told him to take great care of the plates.

12 Q.—Why did the angel give him this warning?

A.—Because he knew that wicked men would try to take them from him.

13 Q.—In what form were the plates?

A.—In the form of a book.

14 Q.—How thick was this book?

A.—About six inches.

15 Q.—How long and how wide was this book?

A.—Nearly eight inches long and about six wide.

16 Q.—How were the plates fastened together?

A.—By three rings, running through all of them.

17 Q.—How thick was each plate?

A.—Not quite as thick as common tin.

18 Q.—Were the plates made of tin?

A.—No, they had the appearance of gold.

19 Q.—What was on these plates?

A.—They were covered with engraved writing.

20 Q.—In what language?

A —In an ancient language, called the reformed Egyptian.

21 Q.—What is this book called?

A.—The Book of Mormon.

22 Q.—Why is it called the Book of Mormon?

A.—Because it was written by the hand of Mormon.

23 Q.—Who was Mormon?

A.—An ancient Nephite prophet.

24 Q.—Who was his son?

A.—The prophet Moroni, who appeared as an angel to Joseph Smith.

25 Q.—Why did Joseph not translate all that was on the plates?

A.—Because some of the plates were sealed.

26 Q.—Will the sealed part ever be translated?

A.—Yes, when the Lord shall direct it to be done.

27 Q.—As Joseph was carrying the plates home, what took place?

A.—Two men attacked him.

28 Q.—Why did they attack him?

A.—They wanted to take the plates from him.

29 Q.—Did they get them?

A.—No; Joseph, being a strong man, got away from these men.

30 Q.—Did any others try to get them?

A.—Yes; mobs often surrounded the house in which he lived.

31 Q.—Did they succeed in obtaining the plates?

A.—No; God preserved them from falling into the hands of the wicked.

32 Q.—Did the wicked try to injure Joseph?

A.—Yes, in many ways.

33 Q.—What were some of those ways?

A.—They tried to shoot him, they made false charges against him, and told all manner of lies about him.

34 Q.—Where was Joseph living at this time?

A.—In the State of New York.

35 Q.—While his life was thus in danger what did he resolve to do?

A.—To remove to the State of Pennsylvania.

36 Q.—When he started for Pennsylvania where did he hide the plates.

A.—In a barrel of beans in his wagon.

37 Q.—When Joseph reached Pennsylvania what did he do?

A.—He began to copy the writings from the plates.

38 Q.—And what then?

A.—To translate them into English.

39 Q.—Who assisted him in this work?

A.—His wife, Emma, Martin Harris and Oliver Cowdery.

40 Q.—To what city did Joseph send a copy of some of the characters?

A.—To New York.

41 Q.—Who took this copy?

A.—Martin Harris.

42 Q.—To whom did he show it?

A.—To Professor Charles Anthon.

43 Q.—Who was Professor Anthon?

A.—A very learned man.

44 Q.—What did the professor say about the characters?

A.—That they were true, and that the translation was correct.

45 Q.—Did he write anything?

A.—Yes, he wrote a certificate to that effect.

46 Q.—Did Martin Harris tell Professor Anthon about the plates?

A.—Yes, that an angel had revealed them.

47 Q.—What did Mr. Anthon then do?

A.—He took the certificate and tore it up.

48 Q.—Why did he do this?

A.—Because he said there is no such thing now as the ministering of angels.

49 Q.—Did he wish to see the plates?

A.—Yes, that he might translate the characters.

50 Q.—When Martin Harris informed him that part of the plates were sealed, what did he say?

A.—That he could not read a sealed book.

51 Q.—By what ancient prophet was this circumstance foretold?

A.—By Isaiah.

52 Q.—In what chapter of Isaiah is this prophecy found?

A.—In the 29th chapter, from the 11th to the 14th verse.

53 Q.—How long ago was it that this prophecy was uttered?

A.—About twenty-six hundred years.

54 Q.—When was it fulfilled?

A.—In April, 1828.

55 Q.—Did Martin Harris show the characters and the translation to anyone else?

A.—Yes, to Dr. Mitchell.

56 Q.—Who was Dr. Mitchell?

A.—A gentleman learned in ancient languages.

57 Q.—What did he say?

A.—The same as Professor Anthon had said, that the characters were true ones, and that the translation was correct.

58 Q,—What did Martin Harris then do?

A.—He returned and wrote for Joseph as he translated.

CHAPTER III.

TRANSLATION TAKEN BY MARTIN HARRIS AND LOST—THE LORD ANGRY—HE TAKES THE PLATES FROM JOSEPH —PLATES RESTORED—AARONIC PRIESTHOOD CONFERRED —BAPTISMS—BOOK OF MORMON COMPLETED—TESTIMONIES TO IT.

1 Q,—What did Martin Harris tease Joseph to let him do?
A.—To take the translation home and show it to his wife and friends.

2 Q.—What did Joseph do?
A.—He enquired of the Lord about the matter.

3 Q.—Did the Lord consent?
A.—Not at first.

4 Q.—When did the Lord permit Martin Harris to take the writings?
A.—Not until Joseph had asked a third time.

5 Q.—In what way did Joseph enquire of the Lord?
A.—Through the Urim and Thummim.

6 Q.—What were the conditions imposed upon Martin Harris.
A.—That he should show the writings to five persons only.

7 Q.—Did Martin Harris bind himself to these conditions?
A.—Yes, with a most solemn promise.

8 Q.—Did he keep his promise?
A.—No.

9 Q.—What was the result?
A.—He lost the writings, and the Lord was angry.

10 Q.—What did the Lord then take from Joseph?
A.—The Urim and Thummim, and soon after the plates.

11 Q.—Were they afterwards restored?
A.—Yes.

12 Q.—Why were they restored?
A.—Because Joseph humbled himself before the Lord.

13 Q.—Who appeared to Joseph Smith and Oliver Cowdery, in the spring of 1829?

A.—John the Baptist.

14 Q.—Upon what day did he appear to them?

A.—On the 15th day of May.

15 Q.—What did he confer upon them?

A.—The Aaronic Priesthood.

16 Q.—Why did God send John the Baptist to do this?

A.—Because he held the keys of this Priesthood.

17 Q.—Who, then, was John the Baptist?

A.—An ancient prophet of God.

18 Q.—Where did he live?

A.—In Judea.

19 Q.—Whom did he baptize?

A.—Jesus Christ, our Savior.

20 Q.—When were Joseph and Oliver baptized?

A.—On the same day that the Aaronic Priesthood was conferred upon them.

21 Q —Who was baptized first?

A.—Oliver Cowdery.

22 Q —Who baptized him?

A.—Joseph Smith.

23 Q.—Who was next baptized?

A.—Joseph Smith.

24 Q.—Who baptized him?

A.—Oliver Cowdery.

25 Q.—What took place next?

A.—Joseph ordained Oliver to the Aaronic Priesthood.

26 Q —And who ordained Joseph Smith?

A.—Oliver Cowdery.

27 Q.—Why did they thus baptize and ordain each other?

A.—Because they were commanded to do so.

28 Q.—What happened after this?

A.— The Holy Ghost fell upon them and they prophesied.

29 Q.—Of what did they prophesy?

A —Of many things that should shortly come to pass.

30 Q.—How long was it after Joseph first saw the Lord that he began to preach?

A.—About nine years.

31 Q.—Why did he not begin before?

A.—Because he had not received the Priesthood.

32 Q.—Had he any right to preach and baptize before he received the Priesthood ?

A.—None whatever:

33 Q.—What is the Priesthood?

A.—It is the power and authority which God gives to men to act in His name.

34 Q.—Where did Joseph complete the translation of the Book of Mormon?

A.—At Father Whitmer's, in Fayette, Seneca County, New York.

35 Q.—When the Book of Mormon was finished, who desired to be witnesses to its truth ?

A.—Oliver Cowdery, David Whitmer and Martin Harris.

36 Q.—Did Joseph enquire of the Lord on this matter? .

A.—Yes.

37 Q.—What answer did the Lord give him ?

A.—That these men should see the plates.

38 Q.—What did the Lord promise that they should see besides the plates of the Book of Mormon ?

A.—The breastplate, the sword of Laban, and the Urim and Thummim.

39 Q.—Were these promises fulfilled ?

A.—Yes.

40 Q.—Who showed them these sacred things ?

A.—An angel, who turned over the leaves of the book before their eyes.

41 Q.—What did the Lord declare to them by His voice?

A.—That the plates had been translated by the gift and power of God.

42 Q.—What did the Lord require of these three witnesses ?

A.—To bear record of what they had seen and heard.

43 Q.—Where can this testimony be found?

A.—In the fore part of the Book of Mormon.

44 Q.—Are there any other witnesses to the truth of the Book of Mormon?

A.—Yes, eight.

45 Q.—Where can their testimony be found?

A.—In the Book of Mormon, immediately below the testimony of the three witnesses.

46 Q.—What is the testimony of these eight witnesses?

A.—That Joseph showed them the plates, and that they handled them.

47 Q.—How many witnesses testified that they saw the plates?

A.—Twelve, including the Prophet, Joseph Smith.

48 Q.—Who printed the first edition of the Book of Mormon?

A —Mr. Egbert Grandon.

49 Q.—Where was it printed?

A.—At Palmyra, Wayne County, New York.

50 Q.—When was it printed?

A —In the latter part of 1829 and the beginning of 1830.

51 Q.—How many copies were then printed?

A.—Five thousand.

52 Q.—What did the printing of this edition cost?

A.—Three thousand dollars.

53 Q.—Were many persons enquiring into the gospel about this time?

A.—Yes, very many.

54 Q.—By whom was the holy apostleship restored to the earth?

A.—Christ's ancient Apostles, Peter, James and John.

55 Q.—Upon whom did they confer this power?

A.—Joseph Smith and Oliver Cowdery.

CHAPTER IV.

CHURCH ORGANIZED—A MIRACLE—JOSEPH SMITH ARRESTED
AND PERSECUTED—FIRST MISSIONARIES—SIDNEY RIGDON
AND OTHERS CONVERTED.

1 Q.—When was the Church of Jesus Christ organized in this dispensation?

A.—On the sixth day of April, 1830.

2 Q.—Who appointed that day?

A.—The Lord.

3 Q.—Where was the Church organized?

A.—In the house of Peter Whitmer, at Fayette, Seneca County, New York.

4 Q.—With how many members was it organized?

A.—Six.

5 Q.—Had more than six persons been baptized up to that date?

A.—Yes, a number more.

6 Q.—Why was the Church organized with six members?

A.—To conform to the laws of that State, which required' at least that number.

7 Q.—How did Joseph know how to organize the Church?

A.—The Lord had revealed it to him.

8 Q.—Who preached the first public discourse after the organization of the Church?

A.—Oliver Cowdery.

9 Q.—When did he preach this discourse?

A.—On Sunday, April 11th, 1830.

10 Q.—Where did he preach it?

A.—In the house of Mr. Whitmer.

11 Q.—What place did Joseph shortly afterwards visit?

A.—Colesville, Broome County, New York.

12 Q.—What happened there?

A.—Joseph, in the name of Jesus Christ, cast an evil spirit out of Newel Knight, which had greatly tormented him

13 Q.—How many witnessed this miracle?

A.—Eight or nine grown persons were in the house at the time.

14 Q.—What effect did this miracle have upon them?

A.—They were astonished at the power of God thus made manifest.

15 Q.—What did they do?

A.—Most of them became members of the Church.

16 Q.—What effect had the circulation of the Book of Mormon among the people?

A.—It was accounted as a strange thing, as foretold by the prophet Isaiah.

17 Q.—What was the name of Joseph's wife before she was married?

A.—Miss Emma Hale.

18 Q.—When were they married?

A.—On the 18th of January, 1827.

19 Q.—When and by whom was she baptized?

A.—In June, 1830, by Oliver Cowdery.

20 Q.—What happened the day Emma Smith was baptized?

A.—Joseph was arrested by a constable.

21 Q.—What charge was made against him?

A.—That he was setting the country in an uproar.

22 Q.—In what way?

A.—By preaching the Book of Mormon.

23 Q.—To what town did the constable take him?

A.—To South Bainbridge, in New York.

24 Q.—Could his accusers prove anything against him?

A.—No, nothing at all.

25 Q.—What did the court do with Joseph?

A.—It acquitted him.

26 Q.—What do you mean by acquitted?

A.—Said he was not guilty, and let him go free.

27 Q.—What next took place?

A —He was again arrested.

28 Q.—By whom?

A.—By a constable from Broome County.

29 Q.—How far did this constable take him?

A.—He took him fifteen miles in a wagon.

30 Q.—Where did they stay?

A.—At a tavern.

31 Q.—What happened there?

A.—A number of men came in, spit upon him, and pointed their fingers at him, saying "Prophesy; prophesy!"

32 Q.—What took place next day?

A.—He was taken before a magistrate and tried.

33 Q.—Was anything evil proved against him?

A.—No; and he was again set a liberty.

34 Q.—Why was Joseph so shamefully persecuted?

A.—Because his religious faith was unpopular with the wicked and ignorant.

35 Q.—Who started these persecutions?

A.—Two leading Presbyterians, named Boyington and McMaster.

36 Q.—Who were the first missionaries appointed to carry the gospel to the Indians?

A.—Oliver Cowdery, Peter Whitmer, Jun., Parley P. Pratt, and Ziba Peterson.

37 Q.—When were they called to this mission?

A.—At a Conference held in September, 1830.

38 Q.—In what direction did these Elders journey?

A.—They traveled from New York to Missouri.

39 Q.—While passing through Ohio whom did they visit?

A.—Sidney Rigdon.

40 Q.—Who was he?

A.—A preacher of the Reformed Baptist Church.

41 Q.—Where did he reside?

A.—At Kirtland.

42 Q.—What did they give him to read?

A.—A copy of the Book of Mormon.

43 Q.—Had he ever seen it before?

A.—No, never.

44 Q.—What else did these Elders do?

A.—They preached to Sidney Rigdon's congregation.

45 Q.—Did any of his congregation believe the gospel?

A.—Yes, seventeen of them.

46 Q.—Did Sidney Rigdon receive it?

A.—Yes; and he and those of his congregation who believed were baptized.

CHAPTER V.

GATHERING THE SAINTS AT KIRTLAND, OHIO, AND JACKSON COUNTY, MISSOURI—OUTRAGES AT HIRAM—POISON GIVEN TO JOSEPH SMITH—BOOKS PRINTED.

1 Q.—Who were the first members of the Church who had the privilege of standing upon ground designed specially for holy purposes?

A.—The four missionary Elders before named.

2 Q.—What place was it?

A.—Independence, Jackson County, Missouri.

3 Q.—What will he built there?

A.—The great temple of Zion.

4 Q.—When and where did Sidney Rigdon first see the Prophet Joseph?

A.—In December, 1830, at Fayette, where Joseph was then living.

5 Q.—Whom did Sidney take with him?

A.—Edward Partridge.

6. Q.—What happened during this visit?

A.—Joseph baptized Edward Partridge.

7 Q.—To what office was he afterwards ordained?

A.—He was the first man ordained a Bishop in the Church.

8 Q.—When Sidney Rigdon and Edward Partridge returned to Kirtland, who went with them?

A.—Joseph Smith and his family.

9 Q.—When did they arrive there?

A.—In February, 1831.

10 Q.—After the prophet Joseph had removed to Kirtland, who else went there?

A.—The Saints from New York and other places.

11 Q.—Why did they go there?

A.—Because the Lord had chosen Kirtland as a Stake of Zion, and a place of gathering.

12 Q.—When did Joseph first visit Jackson County, Missouri?

A.—In July, 1831.

13 Q.—What did the Lord reveal to him about a place called Independence, in that County?

A.—That it is the place where the city of Zion will be built.

14 Q.—What more did He reveal?

A.—That a great temple would be built there.   ʼ

15 Q.—Who else went to Jackson County?

A.—Many families of the Saints went and settled there.

16 Q.—Where was the first building erected by the Saints in that County?

A.—In Kaw Township, twelve miles from Independence.

17 Q.—When was this?

A.—In August, 1831.

18 Q.—How many men carried the first log for the house?

A.—Twelve men, in honor of the twelve tribes of Israel.

19 Q.—Was Joseph Smith one of these twelve men?

A.—Yes.

20 Q.—Was the land consecrated and dedicated to the Lord?

A.—Yes, for a gathering place for the Saints.

21 Q.—Who offered up the dedicatory prayer?

A.—Sidney Rigdon.

22 Q.—When was this?

A.—On the 2nd day of August, 1831.

23 Q.—When was the spot for the building of the temple dedicated?

A.—On the following day, August 3rd.

24 Q.—How many were present at the dedication?

A.—Eight men.

25 Q.—Who offered up the prayer at the dedication of the temple site?

A.—Joseph Smith, the Prophet.

26 Q.—What portion of scripture was read?

A.—The 87th Psalm.

27 Q.—When was the first conference held in Missouri?

A.—On the 4th of August, 1831.

28 Q.—At what place?

A.—In the house of Joshua Lewis, in Kaw Township.

29 Q.—When did Joseph, with some others, start to return to Kirtland?

A.—On the 9th of August, 1831.

30 Q —Where did Joseph and his family remove to?

A.—To Hiram, in Portage County, Ohio.

31 Q.—How far was Hiram from Kirtland?

A.—About thirty miles.

32 Q.—While at Hiram, what duty occupied the Prophet's time and attention?

A.—The translation of the Bible.

33 Q.—When were Joseph Smith and Sidney Rigdon nearly killed by a mob?

A.—On the evening of the 25th of March, 1832.

34 Q.—How did this happen in Joseph's case?

A.—A mob burst into the house of Joseph when he was asleep, and carried him out of doors. They tore off his clothes, and covered him with tar and feathers. They tried to choke him, poison him, and in other ways sought to kill him. But God preserved his life.

35 Q —Who were the leaders of this mob?

A.—Apostates and false professors of religion.

36 Q.—When did Joseph start to revisit the land of Zion?

A.—On the 2nd day of April, 1832.

37 Q.—What happened to Joseph when returning to Kirtland?

A.—Poison was given to him at a tavern in Indiana.

38 Q —What then happened?

A.—He vomited large quantities of blood and poisonous matter, but Brother N. K. Whitney administered to him, and he was instantly healed.

39 Q.—While Joseph was in Independence, Missouri, what was done?

A.—The first edition of the Book of Covenants and Commandments was ordered to be printed.

40 Q.—Was any other book printed about this time?

A.—Yes; a hymn book for the Saints.

41 Q.—What was the title of the newspaper published by the Saints in Independence?

A.—The *Evening and Morning Star.*

42 Q.—When was the first number issued?

A.—In June, 1832.

43 Q.—Was not this the first paper ever published in Upper Missouri?

A.—Yes; its place of publication was 120 miles further west than any other paper published in the United States.

CHAPTER VI.

FIRST MEETING WITH BRIGHAM YOUNG—PREDICTION CONCERNING HIM—SCHOOL OF THE PROPHETS—SAINTS PERSECUTED AND DRIVEN OUT OF MISSOURI—ZION'S CAMP.

1 Q.—When did Joseph start to return to Kirtland?

A.—On the 6th of May, 1832.

2 Q.—Who went with him?

A.—Sidney Rigdon and Newel K. Whitney.

3 Q.—Who visited Joseph at Kirtland in November, 1832?

A.—Brigham Young, Heber C. Kimball and Joseph Young.

4 Q.—Had the Prophet ever seen these brethren before?

A.—No.

5 Q.—During this visit who spoke in tongues?

A.—Brigham Young and John P. Greene.

6 Q.—Had Joseph ever heard any person speak in tongues previous to this?

A.—No; they were the first he ever heard.

7 Q.—Did any others have this gift at the time of this visit?

A.—Yes; the Prophet Joseph, and others.

8 Q.—What did the Prophet Joseph predict concerning President Brigham Young?

A.—That the time would come when he would preside over the whole Church.

9 Q.—When did the Lord give Joseph the revelation concerning the war between the Northern and Southern States?

A.—On the 25th of December, 1832.

10 Q.—At what time did the war in fulfillment of that revelation begin?

A.—Early in 1861.

11 Q.—When did Joseph organize the School of the Prophets, in Kirtland?

A.—In the beginning of 1833.

12 Q.—When did Joseph, as President of the Church, ordain Sidney Rigdon and Frederick G. Williams as his Counselors?

A.—On the 18th of March, 1833.

13 Q.—What else happened at this time?

A.—Many had heavenly visions and saw glorious things.

14 Q.—What troubled the spirit of Joseph about this time?

A —The unwise conduct of some of the Elders and Saints at the gathering place in Missouri.

15 Q --When did the mob commence to persecute the Saints in those parts?

A —In April, 1833.

16 Q.—What did the Jackson County mob do?

A —They killed many of the Saints and drove the rest from their homes.

17 Q.—Who were tarred and feathered by the mob?

A.—Bishop Edward Partridge and some others.

18 Q.—What else did the mob do?

A.—They burned houses and destroyed much property.

19 Q.—When did the women and children flee before the mob?

A.—On the 5th and 6th of November, 1833.

20 Q.—Where did they flee to?

A.—To the wilderness, where they had no shelter for several days.

21 Q.—What was seen on the night of November 13th?

A.—Falling stars appeared in heaven in such numbers that they seemed like a shower of fire.

22 Q.—What effect did this wonderful display have upon the Saints who had been driven from their homes?

A.—It greatly comforted them.

23 Q.—Where did the Saints mostly settle who were driven from Jackson County?

A,—In Clay and Davis Counties, Missouri.

24 Q —When did Joseph take a Mission to Canada and the Eastern States?

A.—In October, 1833.

25 Q.—What great work was in preparation at Kirtland about this time?

A.—The building of a temple.

26 Q.—What did the Prophet Joseph and the Saints do, to have their wrongs redressed?

A.—They petitioned the Governor of Missouri and the President of the United States for redress.

27 Q.—What else did they do?

A.—They sent a letter to Senator Thomas H. Benton, of Missouri, and in other ways sought to bring the facts before the authorities.

28 Q.—Were these efforts successful?

A.—No; neither the State of Missouri nor the general Government would take the necessary steps to restore the people to their homes.

29 Q.—What happened in February, 1834?

A.—Joseph received a command to gather up the strength of the Lord's house, and go up to redeem Zion.

30 Q.—To what position was the Prophet Joseph appointed by a council of Elders before he started on this expedition?

A.—Commander-in-Chief of the armies of Israel.

31 Q.—When did the company leave Kirtland for Missouri?

A.—On the 5th of May, 1834.

32 Q.—By what name is this company known in history?

A.—It is known as Zion's Camp.

33 Q.—When they reached Missouri, how many were there in the company?

A.—About 205 men, besides several women and children.

34 Q.—How was the camp divided?

A.—Into companies of twelve men, with a captain over each company.

35 Q.—Were the brethren of the camp thoroughly united during their travels?

A.—No; some were fault-finding and rebellious.

36 Q.—What was the result of this conduct?

A.—The Lord afflicted the camp with cholera, and thirteen of the brethren died.

37 Q.—When the camp arrived near Clay County, Missouri, who tried to raise an army to fight them?

A.—The leader of a mob, by the name of James Campbell.

38 Q.—What happened to him while crossing the Missouri River?

A.—He and six others were drowned.

39 Q.—What happened when the company were camped between the Little and Big Fishing Rivers.

A.—The Lord sent a terrible storm of hail and rain.

40 Q.—What effect did this storm have upon the mob?

A.—It killed one man and frightened the rest of the mob so that they returned home.

41 Q.—Who were saved and protected by that storm?

A.—The Prophet Joseph and the Saints with him.

42 Q.—How high did the Fishing River rise during the night of the storm?

A.—Nearly forty feet.

CHAPTER VII.

TWELVE APOSTLES CHOSEN—KIRTLAND TEMPLE FINISHED AND DEDICATED—GLORIOUS MANIFESTATIONS—FIRST FOREIGN MISSION.

1 Q.—While Joseph was in Missouri what did he organize there ?

A.—A High Council.

2 Q.—Was this the first High Council organized?

A.—No; one had been organized in Kirtland.

3 Q.—When was the High Council organized in Kirtland?

A.—On the 17th of February previous (1834.)

4 Q.—When was an appeal made by the leading members of the Church to all men, for peace?

A.—In July, 1834.

5 Q —What did Joseph and his brethren propose to buy in Jackson County?

A —The property of the mobbers.

6 Q.—Was their proposal accepted?

A.—No.

7 Q —When did Joseph and others leave Missouri to return to Kirtland?

A.—On July 9th, 1834.

8 Q:—When did they reach Kirtland?

A.—About the 1st of August.

9 Q.—Was the trip from Kirtland to Zion an easy one?

A.—No; it was a fatiguing and trying journey. Many of the brethren walked all the way to Missouri and back.

10 Q.—When was The School of the Prophets again held in Kirtland?

A.—During the latter part of 1834.

11 Q —When were the Twelve Apostles chosen?

A.—On the 14th of February, 1835.

12 Q.—By whom were they chosen?

A.—By the three witnesses to the Book of Mormon.

13 Q.—What are the names of these three witnesses?

A.—Oliver Cowdery, David Whitmer and Martin Harris.

14 Q.—Why did the three witnesses choose the Twelve Apostles?

A.—Because the Lord, by direct revelation, commanded that they should do so.

15 Q.—What were the names of the twelve men thus chosen to form the Quorum of the Twelve Apostles?

A.—Thomas B. Marsh, David W. Patten, Brigham Young, Heber C. Kimball, Orson Hyde, Wm. E. McLellin, Parley P. Pratt, Luke Johnson, Wm. Smith, Orson Pratt, John F. Boynton, and Lyman E. Johnson.

16 Q.—When were the brethren selected who were to form the first quorum of Seventies?

A.—February 28th, 1835.

17 Q.—Who was the First President of all of the Seventies?

A.—Joseph Young.

18 Q.—When did the Twelve Apostles start from Kirtland on their mission to the Eastern States?

A.—In the first week of May, 1835.

19 Q.—Where was the Book of Doctrine and Covenants presented to the Church for its acceptance as a law and rule of faith?

A.—At a general assembly of the Church, held in Kirtland for that purpose?

20 Q.—When was this assembly held?

A.—On the 17th of August, 1835.

21 Q.—Did this assembly accept the book?

A.—Yes, by unanimous vote.

22 Q.—When did Joseph and the leading Elders study Hebrew?

A,—During the winter of 1835-6.

23 Q.—When did Joseph and his counselors first meet in the Kirtland Temple, to attend to the ordinances of washing and anointing?

A.—On the 21st of January, 1836.

24 Q.—Who administered to them there?

A.—Holy angels.

25 Q.—What did the Prophet Joseph see?

A—He saw the Celestial Kingdom of God.

26 Q.—When was the Kirtland temple dedicated?

A.—On Sunday, March 27th, 1836.

27 Q.—Who dedicated the temple with prayer?

A.—The Prophet Joseph Smith.

28 Q.—What holy ordinance was attended to on the Wednesday following?

A.—The ordinance of the washing of feet.

29 Q.—What glorious things were revealed on the next Sunday (April 3rd, 1836)?

A.—The heavens were opened to Joseph Smith and Oliver Cowdery, and the glories thereof were shown to them.

30 Q.—Who appeared to them on this occasion?

A.—Our Lord and Savior, Jesus Christ.

31 Q.—What did He say of Himself?

A.—"I am the first and the last, I am he who liveth, I am he who was slain, I am your advocate with the Father."

32 Q.—After this vision was closed who next appeared?

A.—Moses, the great lawgiver to ancient Israel.

33 Q.—What did he commit to them?

A.—The keys of the gathering of Israel.

34 Q.—Who appeared next?

A.—Elias.

35 Q.—Who appeared after Elias?

A.—The Prophet Elijah, who gave them the keys to turn the hearts of the fathers to the children and the children to the fathers.

36 Q.—Was this in fulfillment of ancient prophecy?

A.—Yes, of prophecies spoken by the mouth of Malachi.

37 Q.—Who were the first Elders sent upon a foreign mission?

A.—Elders Heber C. Kimball, Orson Hyde, Willard Richards and Joseph Fielding.

38 Q.—To what country were they sent?

A.—To England.

39 Q.—When did they leave Kirtland on this mission?

A.—On Tuesday, June 13th, 1837.

40 Q.—When did they sail from New York?

A.—On July 1st, 1837.

41 Q—Who accompanied them from New York?

A.—Elders John Goodson and Isaac Russell and Priest John Snider.

42 Q.—When did they arrive in Liverpool?

A.—On July 20th, and then went on to Preston.

43 Q.—When and where was a meeting held by the mob to take measures to have the Saints driven out of Clay County, Missouri?

A.—At Liberty, June 29th, 1836.

44 Q.—When did the Saints remove and where to?

A.—In the following autumn, to Shoal Creek.

45 Q.—What city did the Saints commence in that region?

A.—The City of Far West, in Caldwell County, Missouri.

46 Q.—When was the ground broken for building a House of the Lord, in that City?

A.—In the beginning of 1837.

CHAPTER VIII.

MISSION TO CANADA—VISIT TO MISSOURI—APOSTASY—ADAM-ONDI-AHMAN—EXTERMINATING ORDER—HAUN'S MILL MASSACRE—JOSEPH BETRAYED—SENTENCED TO BE SHOT —CARRIED TO INDEPENDENCE.

1 Q.—What evil spirit characterized many members of the Church in the summer of 1837?

A.—A spirit of speculation, which was followed by disunion, fault-finding, dissension and apostasy.

2 Q.—Where did Joseph go on a short mission during this summer?

A.—To Canada, where Elder John Taylor was then presiding.

3 Q.—Who went with him?

A.—Sidney Rigdon and Thomas B. Marsh.

4 Q.—When did they return to Kirtland?

A.—About the last day of August.

5 Q.—At what date was a general conference held to reorganize the Church?

A.—On the 3rd of September, 1837.

6 Q.—What took place at this conference?

A.—A number of prominent members of the Church were disfellowshiped.

7 Q.—Shortly after this conference, where did Joseph Smith and Sidney Rigdon go?

A.—To Missouri.

8 Q.—What was the object of their mission?

A.—To find new gathering places for the increasing Saints.

9 Q.—Did Joseph remain long in Missouri?

A.—No; in December he returned to Kirtland.

10 Q.—What was the condition of the Church in Kirtland at that time?

A.—Many had apostatized, and were filled with hatred against the servants of God.

11 Q.—When did Joseph Smith and Sidney Rigdon leave Kirtland to escape mob violence?

A.—On the 12th of January, 1838.

12 Q.—When did they reach Far West?

A.—On the 14th of the next March.

13 Q.—What took place shortly after their arrival?

A.—Some of the Apostles were cut off the Church for transgression.

14 Q.—What was the name of the city about to be built in Daviess County, Missouri.

A.—Adam-ondi-Ahman.

15 Q.—Why was this name given to it?

A.—Because it is the place where Adam will come to visit his people.

16 Q.—What other names are given to Adam in the scriptures?

A.—He is called the Archangel Michael, also the Ancient of Days.

17 Q.—Was a Temple commenced in Far West?

A.—Yes, the corner stones were laid.

18 Q.—When were they laid?

A.—On the of 4th July, 1838.

19 Q.—Who were appointed and ordained to fill the vacancies in the quorum of the Twelve?

A.—Elders John Taylor, John E. Page, Wilford Woodruff, and Willard Richards.

20 Q.—Did persecution soon recommence?

A.—Yes, various brethren were falsely accused and cast into prison.

21 Q.—Who acted as chief persecutor of the Saints?

A.—The infamous Lilburn W. Boggs, governor of the State of Missouri.

22 Q.—What brethren were killed about this time?

A.—Apostle David W. Patten, and Brother Gideon Carter.

23 Q.—Who issued an order to either drive the Saints out of the State of Missouri or kill them?

A.—Governor Boggs.

24 Q.—To whom did he give this order?

A.—To General John B. Clark.

25 Q.—When was this shameful order given?

A.—On the 27th of October, 1838.

26 Q.—What horrible massacre took place within a few days after this order was issued?

A.—The massacre at Haun's mill, in Missouri.

27 Q.—When did this massacre take place?

A.—On Tuesday, October 30th, 1838.

28 Q.—How many of the Saints were killed or mortally wounded at that time?

A.—Eighteen or nineteen.

29 Q.—What is meant by mortally wounded?

A.—Injured so severely as to cause death.

30 Q.—Were there any children killed by the mob at this massacre?

A.—Yes; Sardius Smith, aged fourteen years, and Charles Merrick, aged eight or nine years.

31 Q.—Were there others wounded who afterwards recovered?

A —Yes ; several.

32 Q.—What prominent man in the Church was present at this massacre?

A.—Elder Joseph Young, First President of all the Seventies.

33 Q.—What happened to the Prophet Joseph Smith about this time?

A.—He was taken prisoner with several of his brethren.

34 Q.—By whom was he delivered to the enemy?

A.—By George M. Hinkle, a traitor to the Saints.

35 Q.—What was done to Joseph and his brethren?

A.—They were tried by court martial and sentenced to be shot the next morning.

36 Q.—When this infamous sentence was passed, what did General Doniphan say?

A.—He said that such shooting would be nothing short of cold-blooded murder.

37 Q.—Who was General Doniphan?

A.—One of the chief officers of the militia, who formed the mob.

38 Q.—What effect did this remark have on the other officers?

A.—They determined to take Joseph and the other prisoners to Jackson County.

39 Q.—When did this trial take place?

A.—On the 1st of November, 1838.

40 Q.—By whom where these brethren taken as prisoners?

A.—By the mob, who came to Far West, claiming to be militia of the State.

41 Q.—Where were Joseph and his brethren then taken?

A.—To Independence.

42 Q.—What promise did the Lord grant to Joseph on the way?

A.—That not one of their lives should be taken.

CHAPTER IX.

REMOVAL TO RICHMOND—SAINTS COMPELLED TO LEAVE MISSOURI—SETTLE IN NAUVOO—A MANIFESTATION OF GOD'S POWER—VISIT TO PRESIDENT VAN BUREN.

1 Q.—How long were the captive brethren kept at Independence?

A.—Only a few days.

2 Q.—To what place were they then removed?

A.—To Richmond, Ray County.

3 Q.—How were they treated at Richmond?

A.—They were chained together for several days.

4 Q.—What did the mob do at Far West?

A.—They plundered, abused and ill-treated the Saints in a brutal manner.

5 Q.—When were the Saints compelled to leave Missouri?

A.—In the fall of 1838 and winter of 1838-1839.

6 Q.—Where did the Saints go when they were driven from Missouri?

A.—Into Illinois.

7 Q.—Where was the Prophet Joseph while the Saints were being driven out of Missouri?

A.—He was still kept in chains, and in prison.

8 Q.—Did many of the Saints lose their lives during these mobbings, drivings, and persecutions?

A.—Yes, many, while others were greatly injured in health, and robbed of their property.

9 Q.—To what place in Illinois did the Saints first remove?

A.—To Quincy, on the Mississippi River.

10 Q.—What was their condition when they reached Quincy?

A.—They were in a poor, wretched, and pitiable condition.

11 Q.—How did Joseph instruct the Saints while he was in prison?

A.—He wrote letters to them, containing the word of the Lord, to comfort and cheer them.

12 Q.—Where was Joseph imprisoned at this time?

A.—In Liberty jail, Missouri.

13 Q.—When did he and his brethren escape from prison?

A.—On the evening of April 16th, 1839.

14 Q.—When did they arrive at Quincy?

A.—On Sunday, April 22nd.

15 Q.—What place did Joseph select as the next gathering place of the Saints?

A.—A place on the Mississippi River, called Commerce.

16 Q.—In what County and State was Commerce?

A —In Hancock County, Illinois.

17 Q.—What name did the Saints afterwards give it?

A.—Nauvoo, which means "Beautiful."

18 Q.—How did Joseph obtain possession of Commerce?

A.—There were only six houses there, and he bought them all.

19 Q.—When did Joseph and his family arrive there?

A.—On the 10th of May, 1839.

20 Q. —Was Commerce a healthy place?

A.—No, it was considered very unhealthy.

21 Q.—Was Joseph taken sick?

A.—Yes, and so were many others.

22 Q.—What took place when he was able to get up and walk around?

A.—He went among the sick, healing them by the power of God.

23 Q.—Were many healed?

A.—Yes, in the name of the Lord Jesus Christ.

24 Q.—After healing the sick in Nauvoo, where did he go?

A.—He crossed the Mississippi River to Montrose, Iowa.

25 Q.—What did he do there?

A.—He healed the sick.

26 Q.—Who went with him and assisted him?

A.—Elders Brigham Young, Heber C. Kimball, John Taylor and Wilford Woodruff.

27 Q.—On what day did this great manifestation of God's power and mercy occur?

A.—On the 22nd of July, 1839.

28 Q.—When was the first general conference held at Nauvoo?

A.—On the 5th of October, 1839.

29 Q.—What particular business was done at this conference?

A.—A Stake of Zion was organized, and Elder William Marks appointed its President.

30 Q.—What was decided about Joseph Smith?

A.—That he should go to Washington.

31 Q.—Who were appointed to go with Joseph?

A.—Sidney Rigdon and Elias Higbee.

32 Q.—To whom were they going?

A.—To the President of the United States.

33 Q.—What was his name?

A.—Martin Van Buren.

34 Q.—What was their business with him?

A.—To tell him of the grievous wrongs the Saints had suffered in Missouri, and to ask redress.

35 Q.—When did they arrive in Washington?

A.—On the 28th of November.

36 Q.—When they laid their grievances before President Van Buren, what did he say?

A.—"Your cause is just, but I can do nothing for you."

37 Q.—Did Joseph and his brethren lay the wrongs of the Saints before any other influential men?

A —Yes, before several members of Congress.

38 Q.—Did this have the desired effect?

A.—No; the Saints were not granted redress, so they left their cause in the hands of God.

CHAPTER X.

DOCTRINE OF BAPTISM FOR THE DEAD TAUGHT—HYRUM
SMITH APPOINTED PATRIARCH—NAUVOO LEGION ORGAN-
IZED—NAUVOO TEMPLE COMMENCED—JOSEPH ARRESTED,
TRIED AND SET AT LIBERTY—BAPTISM FOR THE DEAD
PERFORMED—FEMALE RELIEF SOCIETY ORGANIZED—
JOSEPH ARRESTED ON AFFIDAVIT OF GOVERNOR BOGGS
TRIAL AND ACQUITTAL——A PROPHECY.

1 Q.—What was the value of the property of which the
Saints were robbed in Missouri?

A.—Nearly one and a half million dollars.

2 Q.—When did Joseph return to Nauvoo from Washington?

A.—On the 4th of March, 1840.

3 Q.—Who died on the 14th of September, 1840?

A.—Joseph Smith, Senior, the Prophet's father.

4 Q.—What office did he hold?

A.—He was Patriarch to the Church.

5 Q.—When was a resolution passed and a committee
appointed to build a house to the Lord in Nauvoo?

A —At a general conference held in October, 1840.

6 Q —What divine doctrine was taught to the Saints at
this conference?

A.—The doctrine of baptism for the dead.

7 Q.—Who was appointed and ordained Patriarch to the
Church after the death of Father Joseph Smith?

A.- -His eldest son, Hyrum Smith.

8 Q.—What took place on the 30th of January, 1841?

A.—The Prophet Joseph Smith was elected Trustee in
Trust for the Church of Jesus Christ of Latter-day Saints.

9 Q.—When was the Nauvoo Legion organized?

A.—On the 4th of February, 1841.

10 Q.—What office did the Prophet hold in the Legion?

A.—He was lieutenant general.

11 Q—When were the corner stones of the Temple at Nauvoo laid?

A.—On the 6th of April, 1841.

12 Q.—Was Joseph arrested during this year?

A.—Yes, on the 5th of June.

13 Q.—Before whom was he tried?

A.—Before Judge Stephen A. Douglas.

14 Q.—What was the result of the trial?

A —The judge decided he had done nothing worthy of imprisonment, and set him at liberty.

15 Q.—Who instigated this arrest?

A.—The old Missouri mobocrats.

16 Q.—When were baptisms for the dead first performed in the Temple font?

A.—On the 21st of November, 1841.

17 Q.—Who officiated?

A —Elders Brigham Young, Heber C. Kimball and John Taylor baptized, and Elders W. Woodruff, G. A. Smith and Willard Richards, confirmed.

18 Q.—How many did they baptize?

A.—About forty persons.

19 Q.—What society was organized about this time, by the counsel of the Prophet Joseph?

A.—The Female Relief Society of Nauvoo.

20 Q —What took place in May, 1842, that afterwards caused Joseph much trouble and annoyance?

A.—Governor Boggs, of Missouri, was shot at a nd wounded in his own house.

21 Q —Whom did Governor Boggs unjustly charge with this attempt to murder him?

A.—Brother O. P. Rockwell, and that Joseph Smith prompted him to do it, or was accessory before the fact.

22 Q.—What did Governor Boggs do about it?

A.—He had Joseph arrested.

23 Q —Did he accomplish anything by this course?

A.—No; Joseph was set at liberty.

24 Q —What remarkable prophecy did Joseph Smith utter on August 6th, 1842?

A.—That the Saints would continue to suffer much affliction, and would be driven to the Rocky Mountains.

25 Q.—What more did he predict?

A.—That many would apostatize, and others would be put to death by their persecutors, or lose their lives in consequence of exposure and disease.

26 Q.—What did he say about those whose lives would be spared?

A.—That some would go and assist in making settlements and building cities, and see the Saints become a mighty people in the midst of the Rocky Mountains.

27 Q.—What was the public feeling regarding the Saints at that time?

A.— One of great excitement and bitterness.

28 Q.—What did the Lord shortly after reveal to Joseph?

A.—That, for his own safety and that of the people, it would be well for him to leave Nauvoo for a short season.

39 Q.—Did Joseph obey this revelation?

A.—Yes; he went and hid from his enemies for a short time at the houses of different brethren.

30 Q.—Of what periodical was Joseph the editor at this time?

A.—The *Times and Seasons*, published at Nauvoo.

31 Q.—Whom did Joseph appoint to succeed him in editing the *Times and Seasons*?

A.—Elders John Taylor and Wilford Woodruff.

32 Q.—Did Joseph suffer any more annoyance from Governor Boggs' false charge?

A.—Yes; he was arrested a second time, on the 26th of December, 1842.

33 Q.—Where was he taken?

A.—To Springfield, Illinois.

34 Q.—When did his trial take place?

A.—On the 4th of January, 1843, before Judge Pope.

35 Q —Was he found guilty?

A.—No; he was proven innocent of the charges made against him.

36 Q.—When did he return to Nauvoo?

A.—On the 10th of January 1843.

———•▶━◀•———

CHAPTER XI.

JOSEPH KIDNAPPED—RELEASED BY FRIENDS—REVELATION
ON CELESTIAL MARRIAGE—A PROPHECY—OUTRAGES BY
MOB—MARTIAL LAW IN NAUVOO.

1 Q.—When preaching in the temple on January 22nd, 1843, what remarkable statement did Joseph make?

A.—He said, "I shall not be sacrificed until my time comes, and then I shall be offered freely."

2 Q.—What office in the city government did Joseph Smith hold?

A.—That of mayor.

3 Q.—What happened to Joseph in June, 1843?

A.—He was arrested while on a visit to his wife's sister, near Dixon, Lee County, Illinois.

4 Q.—By whom was he arrested?

A.—Sheriff Reynolds and Constable Wilson, from Missouri.

5 Q.—How did they treat him?

A.—With much abuse and cruelty.

6 Q.—What did they endeavor to do with Joseph?

A.—To carry him to Missouri, without any legal right to do so.

7 Q.—Did they succeed?

A.—No; his friends interposed in his behalf, and he was returned to Nauvoo, to the great joy of the Saints.

8 Q.—What was done with him when he reached Nauvoo?

A.—He was tried and acquitted by the municipal court of Nauvoo.

9 Q.—Was this action legal under the laws of Illinois?

A.—It was.

10 Q.—When was the revelation on celestial marriage first written?

A.—On the 12th of July, 1843.

11 Q.—Was this the first time the word of the Lord had been given to Joseph on this important subject?

A.—No; he had been taught the principle by the Lord several years previously.

12 Q.—When was the Nauvoo Mansion opened?

A.—About the middle of September, 1843.

13 Q.—What was the general feeling of the people in Missouri and Illinois towards Joseph and the Saints about this time?

A.—It was that of bitter hatred.

14 Q.—What took place in the city council on the 29th of December, 1843?

A.—Forty men were sworn in as city police.

15 Q.—After they had taken the oath of office, who gave them instructions?

A.—Joseph Smith, the Prophet.

16 Q.—Why were so many policemen needed?

A.—Because Joseph Smith's life was constantly threatened by apostates and others.

17 Q.—What was done on the 17th of February, 1844.

A.—A meeting was held at Carthage for the purpose of having the Saints driven from Nauvoo.

18 Q.—What prediction did Joseph Smith make on the 25th of February?

A.—That in five years the Saints would be beyond the reach of their enemies.

19 Q.—Was that prophecy fulfilled?

A.—Yes; thousands of Saints were in Salt Lake City within that time.

20 Q.—For what object was an important meeting held at the temple on the 7th of March?

A.—To continue the work on the temple.

21 Q.—Who were present at the meeting?

A.—The Prophet Joseph, his brother Hyrum, eight of the Twelve Apostles and eight thousand Saints.

22 Q.—When did Joseph Smith offer himself as a candidate for the office of President of the United States?

A.—In the spring of 1844.

23 Q.—Who became one of the leading apostates about this time?

A.—William Law, who had been one of Joseph's counselors.

24 Q.—What happened on Sunday, April 28th, 1844?

A.—A number of apostates met at the house of Wilson Law, to try to establish a new church.

25 Q.—What commenced shortly after?

A.—Acts of violence and murder by the mob against the Saints.

26 Q.—Where?

A.—In the small settlements, where the Saints were not strong enough to defend themselves.

27 Q.—What was the intention of the mobbers as soon as they could obtain aid from Missouri?

A.—To capture Joseph and destroy the city of Nauvoo.

28 Q.—When Joseph learned of these wicked plans, what did he do?

A.—He placed guards in and around the city, to protect it.

29 Q.—Who was governor of Illinois in 1844?

A.—Thomas Ford.

30 Q.—Did Joseph write to Governor Ford?

A.—Yes; asking him to come to Nauvoo and learn the truth regarding the causes of the trouble.

31 Q.—When was martial law declared in Nauvoo?

A.—On the 18th of June, 1844.

32 Q.—Why was it declared?

A.—To protect the citizens.

33 Q.—Did the governor go to Nauvoo?

A.—No; but he went to Carthage, eighteen miles distant, where the mob had gathered.

34 Q.—What did the governor do when he arrived at Carthage?

A.—He sent an express to the mayor and city council of Nauvoo.

35 Q.—What did he wish?

A.—One or more persons to be sent to Carthage to tell him about the difficulties.

36 Q.—Who were sent?

A.—Elders John Taylor and John M. Bernhisel.

37 Q.—What did they take with them?

A.—Papers containing an account of the doings of the mob.

38 Q.—Did Joseph again request the governor to come to Nauvoo?

A.—Yes, in a second letter, but the governor did not do so.

39 Q.—Why did he not go to Nauvoo?

A.—Because he had become friendly with the mob, and they were anxious that he should not learn the truth by going to Nauvoo.

CHAPTER XII.

"NAUVOO EXPOSITOR" ABATED AS A NUISANCE—JOSEPH'S
RESOLVE—INDUCED TO ABANDON IT—APOSTLES CALLED
HOME—STATE ARMS DEMANDED—GOES TO CARTHAGE—
DUPLICITY OF FORD.

1 Q.—What paper did the apostates in Nauvoo begin to publish in June, 1844?

A.—The *Nauvoo Expositor.*

2 Q.—What was the nature of its contents?

A.—It contained all manner of lies about and abuse of Joseph and the Saints.

3 Q.—What did the city council do in regard to this paper?

A.—It declared it a nuisance, and as such ordered it to be abated.

4 Q.—How was the order carried out?

A.—The city marshal and several policemen threw the printing press, type, etc., into the street and destroyed them.

5 Q.—What was the result of this act?

A.—It caused great excitement among the wicked, and they sought the life of Joseph and the destruction of Nauvoo.

6 Q —What next did Governor Ford require of Joseph and the city council?

A.—That they should go to Carthage to be tried for destroying the *Expositor* printing office.

7 Q.—What prophetic remark did Joseph make to Stephen Markham respecting himself and his brother Hyrum?

A.—That if they were taken again they would be killed.

8 Q.—Under these trying circumstances what did Joseph resolve to do?

A.—To start for the Rocky Mountains.

9 Q.—When did he do this?

A.—On the evening of the 22nd of June.

10 Q.—What took place the next morning?

A.—A company of men came from Carthage to Nauvoo to arrest Joseph.

11 Q.—Did Joseph carry out his design of going to the Rocky Mountains?

A.—No; at the solicitation of his wife, Emma, and others he returned to Nauvoo.

12 Q.—Was this course agreeable to Joseph's own feelings?

A.—No; he expressed the opinion that it would result in his death.

13 Q.—What did he say?

A.—"If my life is of no value to my friends, it is of none to myself."

14 Q.—What else did he say?

A.—"We shall be butchered."

15 Q.—When Joseph returned to Nauvoo what offer did he make Governor Ford?

A —To go to Carthage if he would send men to guard him and would secure him a fair trial.

16 Q.—What word did Joseph send to the Twelve who were upon missions?

A.—To come home immediately, on account of trouble.

17 Q.—Did Governor Ford send the guard Joseph asked for?

A.—No; but sent a message for him to be at Carthage at ten o'clock the next morning.

18 Q.—Did Joseph go?

A.—Yes, accompanied by eighteen brethren.

19 Q.—Whom did the party meet on the road?

A.—Captain Dunn, with a party of sixty mounted militia.

20 Q.—What did Captain Dunn present to Joseph?

A.—An order from Governor Ford for all the State arms in possession of the Nauvoo Legion.

21 Q.—What did Joseph then do?

A.—He countersigned the order (or signed it himself) and returned to Nauvoo to see that the arms were given up.

22 Q.—When the fire-arms were given up, what did Joseph do?

A.—After bidding his family farewell, he again started for Carthage.

23 Q.—When opposite the Masonic Hall, what did he say to some brethren there?

A:—"Boys, if I don't come back, take care of yourselves; I am going like a lamb to the slaughter."

24 Q.—When did Joseph and the brethren arrive at Carthage?

A.—About midnight.

25 Q.—While they were passing the public square, what threats did some of the soldiers make?

A.—They threatened to shoot Joseph, and said he would never see Nauvoo again.

26 Q.—On what charge were Joseph and Hyrum arrested the next morning?

A.—On a charge of treason.

27 Q.—What pledge, or promise, did Governor Ford make to Joseph?

A.—That he would protect him and his friends from violence.

28 Q.—When Joseph was visited by a number of the officers of the troops, what did he tell them?

A.—He told them they thirsted for his blood, and nothing short of it would satisfy them.

29 Q.—Did Joseph and Hyrum and the brethren stand their trial on the charge of treason?

A.—Yes; but it was all a sham, and only done to try to send them to jail.

30 Q.—Who went to Governor Ford to try to persuade him not to let Joseph and others be sent to jail contrary to law?

A.—Elder John Taylor.

31 Q.—Did he succeed?

A.—No; the governor utterly refused to interfere in their behalf.

32 Q.—Who then went as a guard with Joseph and Hyrum to prison?

A.—John Taylor, Stephen Markham, Dan Jones and three others.

33 Q.—How did they spend the evening in Carthage jail?

. A.—In pleasant conversation and in prayer.

34 Q.—What did Joseph do the next morning?

A.—He wrote a letter to Governor Ford, complaining of the illegal treatment to which they were subjected.

35 Q.—What reply did the governor make?

A.—That he would protect them against violence.

36 Q.—How did Joseph and the brethren spend their time during the day?

A.—In writing, singing, relating dreams, etc.

37 Q.—Where was Joseph taken in the afternoon?

A.—To the court house, to have his trial.

38 Q.—Did his trial take place that afternoon?

A.—No; it was put off till the next day.

39 Q.—What news did Joseph learn in the evening?

A.—That the governor and all the troops except fifty would march to Nauvoo at eight o'clock the next morning.

CHAPTER XIII.

PRISONERS IN JAIL—ASSASSINATED—JOSEPH AND HYRUM
SMITH KILLED AND JOHN TAYLOR WOUNDED.

1 Q.—What did Joseph do on the morning of June 27th
1844?

A.—He wrote letters to his wife, and to his lawyers.

2 Q.—What occurred about five o'clock in the afternoon?

A.—There was a rustling at the outer door of the jail,
and a discharge of fire arms.

3 Q.—Who were with Joseph and Hyrum in the jail?

A.—Elders John Taylor and Willard Richards.

4 Q.—Who were on the outside?

A.—About one hundred armed men, around the door of
the jail.

5 Q.—What did some of them do?

A.—Some fired in through the windows, and others ran
up stairs and began firing.

6 Q.—What then happened?

A.—Hyrum Smith received several shots, and as he fell
he said, "I am a dead man."

7 Q.—Who was the next that was shot by these murderers?

A.—President John Taylor, who was wounded in four or
five places.

8 Q.—When Joseph saw there was no safety in the room,
what did he do?

A.—He sprang to the window, intending to leap from it
to the ground.

9 Q.—What happened then?

A.—Three bullets pierced his body, and he fell outward
into the yard, dead.

10 Q.—What did he exclaim after he was shot?

A.—"O Lord, my God."

11 Q.—What was done by the mob after he had fallen from the window?

A.—Joseph was lifted up and placed against the curb of a well.

12 Q.—What did Williams, the commander of the mob order?

A.—He ordered four men to shoot him.

13 Q.—Did they do so?

A.—Yes; they stood about eight feet from the well. and all fired at once.

14 Q.—What was done next?

A.—A man with a bowie knife raised his hand to cut off Joseph's head.

15 Q.—What prevented him committing this brutal outrage?

A.—A vivid flash of lightning caused his arm to fall powerless.

16 Q.—What became of Dr. Richards during this murderous attack?

A.—He escaped unhurt, in a most miraculous manner.

17 Q.—And what became of Elder John Taylor?

A.—Though severely wounded, he recovered after a long sickness and much suffering.

18 Q.—What did the mob do after they had murdered Joseph and Hyrum?

A.—They all fled from Carthage.

19 Q.—Why did they thus flee?

A.—Because they feared the just vengeance of the Saints.

20 Q.—Did the Saints take revenge on the murderers?

A.—No; they left them in the hands of God, who has said, "Vengeance is mine, I will repay."

21 Q.—How old was the Patriarch, Hyrum Smith, when he was martyred?

A.—Forty-four years.

22 Q.—And how old was Joseph the Prophet?

A.—Thirty-eight years.

23 Q.—What was the date of their martyrdom?

A.—The 27th of June, 1844.

24 Q.—Have any of those wicked men ever been punished by the law of the land for this cruel murder?

A.—No; not one.

25 Q.—What became of the bodies of Joseph and Hyrum?

A.—They were taken to Nauvoo the morning after they were killed.

26 Q.—Who went out of Nauvoo to meet them?

A.—Nearly all the people of the city.

27 Q.—To what place were they taken?

A.—To the Nauvoo Mansion, Joseph's late residence, where over ten thousand people came to look at them.

28 Q.—Where were they buried?

A.—They were privately buried in Nauvoo.